IT'S TIME TO EAT CABBAGE

It's Time to Eat CABBAGE

Walter the Educator

Silent King Books
A WhichHead Entertainment Imprint

Copyright © 2024 by Walter the Educator

All rights reserved. No part of this book may be reproduced in any manner whatsoever without written per- mission except in the case of brief quotations embodied in critical articles and reviews.

First Printing, 2024

Disclaimer

This book is a literary work; the story is not about specific persons, locations, situations, and/or circumstances unless mentioned in a historical context. Any resemblance to real persons, locations, situations, and/or circumstances is coincidental. This book is for entertainment and informational purposes only. The author and publisher offer this information without warranties expressed or implied. No matter the grounds, neither the author nor the publisher will be accountable for any losses, injuries, or other damages caused by the reader's use of this book. The use of this book acknowledges an understanding and acceptance of this disclaimer.

It's Time to Eat CABBAGE is a collectible early learning book by Walter the Educator suitable for all ages belonging to Walter the Educator's Time to Eat Book Series. Collect more books at WaltertheEducator.com

USE THE EXTRA SPACE TO TAKE NOTES AND DOCUMENT YOUR MEMORIES

CABBAGE

It's time to eat, come gather around,

It's Time to Eat Cabbage

Cabbage is crunchy, what a sound!

Green or purple, round and tight,

On the table, it's such a sight.

Peel the leaves, so soft and smooth,

Chop it up, it's time to groove.

Into the bowl or in a pan,

Cabbage is part of a yummy plan.

It's fun to eat, it's fun to crunch,

We can have cabbage for dinner or lunch.

With carrots and dressing, make it a slaw,

A tasty dish to make you go "Aww!"

Cook it in soup, or steam it hot,

Cabbage is yummy, we love it a lot!

Wrap it up with rice or meat,

A cabbage roll is such a treat.

Cabbage grows in the sunshine bright,

Farmers pick it when it's just right.

In the garden, it sits so proud,

A leafy ball under a green cloud.

It's full of goodness, vitamins too,

It's Time to Eat
Cabbage

Cabbage helps take care of you!

For growing tall and feeling great,

Cabbage is food that's first-rate.

It's time to share, so take a bite,

Chew it up, it feels just right.

Crunchy and fresh, or soft and sweet,

Cabbage is always a fun food to eat.

With a little salt, or on a plate,

Cabbage can make your meal first-rate.

In a stir-fry or in a stew,

Cabbage is ready to please me and you.

So, let's all cheer for cabbage today,

Healthy and tasty in every way.

Time to eat, let's dig right in,

Cabbage is where the fun begins!

Now clap your hands and stomp your feet,

Cabbage is a veggie that can't be beat.

Every leaf is a little surprise,

It's Time to Eat
Cabbage

Time to eat cabbage, it's so wise!

ABOUT THE CREATOR

Walter the Educator is one of the pseudonyms for Walter Anderson. Formally educated in Chemistry, Business, and Education, he is an educator, an author, a diverse entrepreneur, and he is the son of a disabled war veteran. "Walter the Educator" shares his time between educating and creating. He holds interests and owns several creative projects that entertain, enlighten, enhance, and educate, hoping to inspire and motivate you. Follow, find new works, and stay up to date with Walter the Educator™ at WaltertheEducator.com

Milton Keynes UK
Ingram Content Group UK Ltd.
UKHW010227111224
452348UK00011B/548